JOURNEY LATE AT NIGHT
Poems & Translations

Leo Yankevich

Books by Leo Yankevich

Collections
The Unfinished Crusade
The Last Silesian
Tikkun Olam (second edition)

Chapbooks
The Language of Birds
Grief's Herbs (after Stanisław Grochowiak)
The Gnosis of Gnomes
Epistle from the Dark
The Golem of Gleiwitz

E-Books
Metaphysics
"You Who Live and Hear"
Tikkun Olam (first edition)

JOURNEY LATE AT NIGHT
Poems & Translations

Leo Yankevich

Counter-Currents Publishing Ltd.
San Francisco
2013

Cover image:
Ivan Aivazovsky, "Pushkin in Gurzuf"

Cover design by Kevin I. Slaughter

Published in the United States by
COUNTER-CURRENTS PUBLISHING LTD.
P.O. Box 22638
San Francisco, CA 94122
USA
http://www.counter-currents.com/

Hardcover ISBN: 978-1-935965-82-4
Paperback ISBN: 978-1-935965-83-1
E-book ISBN: 978-1-935965-84-8

Library of Congress Cataloging-in-Publication Data

Yankevich, Leo.
  [Poems. Selections]
  Journey Late at Night : Poems & Translations / Leo
Yankevich.
      pages cm
  ISBN 978-1-935965-82-4 (hardcover : alk. paper) -- ISBN
978-1-935965-83-1 (pbk. : alk. paper) -- ISBN 978-1-935965-
84-8 (electronic book)
  I. Title.

PS3625.A6795A6 2013
811'.6--dc23

2013033206

Acknowledgments

Some of the poems in this collection first appeared in the following journals:

Amelia, American Jones Building & Maintenance, Artword Quarterly, The Barefoot Muse, Beauty for Ashes Poetry Review, Blue Unicorn, Candelabrum, Cedar Hill Review, The Chimaera, Chronicles: A Magazine of American Culture, Counter-Currents/North American New Right, Counter-Punch, Disquieting Muses, The East River Review, Edge City Review, Electric Acorn, The Eclectic Muse, Envoi, The Flea, FutureCycle Poetry, Harpstrings, The HyperTexts, Iambs & Trochees, The Innisfree Poetry Journal, Iota, Ironwood, Kimera, Lite: Baltimore's Literary Newspaper, Loch Raven Review, The London Magazine, Lucid Rhythms, The MacGuffin, The Monongahela Review, Mr. Cogito, The Neovictorian/Cochlea, New Hope International, Nostoc, Parnassus Literary Journal, Pennine Platform, The Pennsylvania Review, The Pittsburgh Post-Gazette, Poetry Nottingham, Poetry Salzburg, Psychopoetica, Raintown Review, Riverrun, Romantics Quarterly, The Sarmatian Review, Ship of Fools, The Shit Creek Review, Snakeskin, Shatter Colors Literary Review, Sonnet Scroll, Staple, Sulphur River Literary Review, Tennessee Quarterly, The Tennessee Review, Tucumcari Literary Review, Trinacria, Visions International, Weyfarers, Whelks Walk Review, Windsor Review, inter alia.

CONTENTS

I. Poems

II. Translations

POEMS

A December Wish

You hear the sound of carols from afar.
Bright bulbs and tinsel, cinnamon and cloves.
Beyond a hill of snow you see a star.

Here you can look at stacks of Christmas trees,
buy nuts and raisins, fruit from nearby groves,
cards inscribed in gold: "joy, love and peace."

And you can eat kielbasa from a spit
as fat drips sizzling in makeshift stoves
and zlotys are exchanged and butts are lit.

Here you can watch fat women slaughter fish
if you stand in the line and bear the shoves,
pretending that you really have a wish.

And for a moment you can close your eyes
and can forget the cold that pierces gloves
and see a diamond necklace in the skies,

or Jesu here among the city doves.

A Tiny Glow

Without the moon or stars to guide his sight,
without a glint from shanties down below,
he rested on the foggy hill that night, and
begged the heavens for a tiny glow.

Despair turned into dream . . . a little boat
with fishermen inside in search of faith,
a boat which, neither sinking nor afloat,
now blindly drifted past a drowning wraith.

And he among them, but incapable
of seeing a reflection in the waves,
which lapped against the stormy parable
like hammers beating iron into staves.

But when he woke at dawn his eyes could see
light walking on the dew toward Galilee.

After Twenty Years of Marriage

Here is a river with a little boat
moored beside its bank. The boat's the colour
of oranges in the south of Greece, all bloody
and ripe with sweetness, while the bank's the colour
of meadows in the north of France, deep green
with a heifer's downy mane, a country rose.
Love, I shall never take you to those places.
I've squandered all my gold upon the water,
which for you mirrors the eternal sun.

Ah, Love

Though many years have passed, and loves, I swear
I can still smell the soaps this one would use.
I can still see the mole on her left thigh,
black Eden lace against her northern skin.

And I recall the thong straps she would wear,
the camisoles and fishnets she would choose,
brown archipelago in her blue eye,
and how she opened doors and let me in.

My lover in her room—a universe
of small particulars: the way she moaned,
the way she hinted which of us was worse,

my lust-shorn shorts beside the book she'd loaned,
and later verbal cruelties, each curse,
and silence after she no longer phoned.

Angel

To wake again like dew upon the blades
of the green meadow, like a gust of wind
pushing the clouds above the forest glades,
at last free from desire, no longer pinned

to gristle, sinews and a skeleton.
To wake again, the water underwing
blue grey until the morning shore and sun,
the crowns of elms and oaks now wavering,

the pearly gate inhuman and aglow
upon the mossy hill, the crystal forms
embracing April rain, the drainage flow
flushing flotsam in the wake of storms.

At a Suicide's Grave (1869–1897)

Here where this graveyard comes to a sudden end
you lie forgotten beside a crumbling wall,
yet sometimes at night a nova calls you friend,
and the moon itself recalls your rise and fall.

Babcia

Milk curdles in her jar,
mould forms on her black bread.
She's come so very far,
but her blue Polish eyes
no longer see the flies
buzzing above her head.

She does not hear her friend
knocking at the door.
This is her journey's end,
the faithful silly dear.
Christ does not shed a tear,
not for the meek and poor.

He looks down from the wall,
with both arms open, heart
sacred, eyes blind to all,
truly not of this world.
He does not see her curled-
up broken flesh depart,

resurrected by
the hour towards the skies.
He won't feed her a lie,
nor redeem a bone.
He will leave her alone
in the kingdom where she lies.

Baroque Nativity Scene

Malachite of tower and dome,
clatter of sabots, creaks of wheels,
neighs of horses headed home
from a market where smoked eels

glimmer in the October sun.
As merchants hawk their sundry wares
an English poet, squire John Donne,
stands by a basket full of pears.

Clad in a purple gown, a tart
straight out of Caravaggio
offers smiles for the sake of art,
and Rubenesquely curtsies low.

She is the virgin mother of Christ,
albeit in one timeless pose.
Pious, but easily enticed,
will he kneel to take off her clothes?

Beast

It's night again. Above the dreaming hill
stars are so close your finger reaches them.
You've downed your pint of beer, have had your fill
of darts and cards, and piss beneath a stem
of cherry blossom. Luna's in your eyes
and speaks a language only you can hear,
a language of hermetic grunts and sighs.
You know a beast is stalking, and a deer
is running for its life a breath away.
You are a bit of both, you think, with feet
now moving toward the shanty in the dale
like hooves of an uneasy woodland stray,
or paws of a wolf that trails a distant bleat
until its muzzle finds your bushy tail.

Beasts

How many beasts
had roamed the soil
before man's feasts
began to spoil
their habitat?
Eat or be eaten?
Even the fat
from a club-beaten
dhole was treasured,
its snout and tongue
crudely measured
with fists, then flung,
into a kettle
chipped out of stone.
A jell would settle.
Headcheese alone
helped cause the death
of many species
of which man's breath,
brain, and feces
are not of any
greater worth.
Think of the many
that walked the earth.

Bethlehem

They come, come faithfully to behold him,
three kings and their harems after three nights
of fasting, coated in an afterlife
of sweet confection. But the star is dim

in the baker's eyes. Camels and a roan
forever near the marzipan manger,
and in the otherworldly glaze, danger
is as heavy as a sepulchral stone.

Indeed, no mouse made of raisin can budge
still eternity to suddenly move
a disfigured nostril or candied hoof.

And the unborn child? How long can it fudge
salvation as sprinkled-white Mary waits
for all that's to come to never take place?

Billie

I felt it in her body loves ago.
Call it what you will: her psyche, soul,
essence, the ghost I never got to know
that haunts me down my later years. A fool,
I wanted flesh, her buttocks and the small
of her back bent beneath my thrusts, her red
dress open, chestnut hair against the wall,
creamy face pressed deep into the bed
till climax and exhaustion merged with dawn.
I could please her, but could not keep her long.
Three binges later she was packed and gone,
her scent still married to my skin, her song
so like a sparrow's in my trembling hand,
a song I could not free, or understand.

Black Oak

At midnight, just beneath the sunken moon,
there is a glade, where leaf on fallen leaf
lie underneath her long and bony arms.
There, naked, she awaits her time to come.
But, singing in her way a mournful tune
of many years gone by, of death and grief,
of olden incantations, herbs, and charms,
she never moves on, only gestures some
to frightened voles and sage and sleepless owls.
You crouch and watch amid ferns, ill at ease
at what you see: a crow's eye of a ditch;
and what you hear: her consonants and vowels
caught and carried far off by the breeze.
And for a moment you think: she's a witch.

Blurb

You take the book from the shelf,
hold it in your hand,
crack it open, leaf
through pages, stop at a line:

a waste of paper, of trees,
of lumberjacks' painful work—
each blurb on the back, a kiss
on the butt of modern verse.

Break of Dawn

I rise at the break of dawn,
still dreaming, half awake,
wondering whether I'm gone;
but, the sun on the lake,

the ancient stones, the pine-trees,
and the mad hungry birds
(in a language without words
borne to me by the breeze)

softly utter, "No,
on and on you must go;
this life do what you can;
eternity has no end."

Brother,

I can still hear your voice
although decades have passed—
the baritone of a man
who is approaching fifteen.

Knees and knuckles numb,
you stand on the snowy bank
of the Shenango River,
pulling an angry muskrat
from an old steel trap.

Like a Eucharist
you hold it up against
the Pennsylvania sky,
its only remaining paw
bleeding, almost severed,
dangling in the sun.

Blue-lipped and barely eight,
I shiver in the wind,
and almost weep for home.

"It made it all this way"—
you say—"on three raw bones,
and still defies its death,
just like we must the cold."

Burn

Better than the burn of booze
when Jack Frost penetrates your bone
is the cheap skid-row wine you use
to light the day when you're alone.

As spleen and liver give up ghosts
the leaves go golden on their stems,
then fall before the lord of hosts
who neither cares, saves, nor condemns.

The hand of the grandfather clock
moves you towards a grotto grave,
while you lie ready by the rock
or say goodbye beneath a wave.

Clarity

This God-gifted dawn,
dawn of brilliant leaves
and dew-dampened clover—

wakes the drowsy senses,
telling them to proclaim
joy and adoration.

But the mind sees beetles
slain along a path,
and wishes for more clarity.

Communion

Where paint peels in the summer sun,
I sit down on the wino bench,
a sinner who must break a bun
to stay alive. I ask: whose stench

is it here, ghost or spirit come
and gone, like draughts of air beneath
the wings of mourning doves? I'm dumb
before the flowering Spanish heath.

The beasts within my belly bay,
themselves but shadows in the dark.
Yet I am made whole by the ray
that lights the pathway in the park.

Cracow

This dawn of fog and lingering dreams, you feel
the centuries in your waking body. Cracow
lies on a river at the foot of a hill.
Light and bells awaken senses. Black now
in shadows, hawkers fill the market square.
Pigeons greet your nose and eyes, and flowers.
You give a gnarly woman coins, and stare
up at the sky, and see the fairy towers,
the malachite-green roofs, above which rooks
fly north from Brno, Prague, or Budapest.
A fiddler plays his violin, and looks
up toward you, knowing you're too soft and green
to pass him by. Your senses cannot rest.
The day begins, old, musty and serene.

Cracow at Dawn

1.

Beneath the clouds
in the corner of my faithless eyes
seven magpies have stolen away
the morning star.
Glory, glory! The rising sun
crowns the cathedral
in this town stopped still
in awe of blazing malachite.
Reborn are the winged shades
in the rookeries
to haunt dear heaven
with their pained pterodactyl cries.
Reborn are the grey pigeons
on the old market square
quarrelling with their enemies,
the dirty sparrows.

2.

Sancho, my old friend,
is it time to embrace more love,
to sit with the ageing harlots
mid the pews of Saint Anne,
though the heft on our backs
is heavier than the rood,
than the silent sermons
of characters stained in glass?

I've two coins in my pocket
as poisonous as lead,
enough for a flask of rum
or Hungarian wine.
Let's park our gaunt donkey
beneath the Baroque clouds,
then limp back to the inn
for as long as there is time . . .

Creature in the Corn

My grandson sees a creature in the corn,
a wolf at odds with fate, paws clasped in prayer.
Today he will have more than thin despair,
than dreams inside a kettle, old and worn.
He does not know the pain of being born
into real hunger, enough to know its stare,
how wolves will jump to snap their teeth at air
from which the ghosts of ptarmigan are torn.
My grandson dreams an end to every tale:
The hungry wolf will find new kinds of prey,
having left for good through fields of gold
to feast on fishes in a living well.
My grandson eats my words, although I pray
he'll never know the taste of bitter cold.

Crossing Geneva Marsh

Mist lingers on the surface
of stagnant tea-brown water.
The flat bridge spans a mile,
a sea of spatterdocks.

Tangled stalks of cattails
and swamp grass reach up towards
the underside of the deck,
the chalcedony of cloud.

My father's at the wheel of
his coffin Cadillac,
following a wayward crow
into the depths of autumn.

His headlights gaze into
the Nietzschean abyss.
And then the same abyss
gazes back into us.

Rear tail-fins cut through
the snapping-turtle air,
past the scarlet oaks
and shagbark hickories.

Smoke from his cigar
drifts out his cracked window,
heavenward, as we head
towards the exit at Mercer.

We turn in the direction
of Farrell, Sharon, Youngstown,
and pass the furnaces
of purgatory and hell.

Crow

Crow, the doves descending on the square
have sullied your name, cooed gossip to wealthy tourists,
their gullets stuffed with handouts, while you soar
over the oaks with dreaming clouds, with the glare
and glimmer of the distant but holy sun
in your misunderstood eyes, your paeans one
with the wind. Yet it was you who, perched on the shoulder
of Jesus, watched him suffer and heard him cry,
and it was you who saw the enormous boulder
moved, and you who saw him enter the sky.

Despair

Alone in the dark, the blood of blackberries
dripping down his shins, the morning star
looking back in the mirror through which he gazes,

moon-eyed and at odds with himself, he presses
his palms, but the nightmare doesn't stop.
The sky turns and nothing this moment matters.

Not even the cold thorns of the blind wind
blowing hellward, not even the poisoned rainbow
that lights his prayers can give meaning to doubt.

The sullen belladonna that pricks his mind
will not comfort him in this final hour
and no guardian angel will come to touch his brow.

Don Quixote

Suddenly, I am astride a donkey
with Sancho Panza. As usual, my head
is in the clouds. And I am stubborn, stupid
as always. Please forgive my making so
much noise when I send dreams to tap against
your window-pane. I've come prepared this time.

When you say that you never loved me,
I kiss your feet. When you say that you fear me,
I kiss your knees, your pale and precious knees.
By this time you expect me to have brought
a single rose, reflecting northern skies.
But no, I've brought the best Swiss chocolate,

rife with exotic fruit and hazelnuts.
You turn your face away, embarrassed to
have been acquainted with my person. So
I settle for the shadow of your neck.
Then I move down and kiss your noble arms,
which tower like two queens above a servant.

I kiss your belly, and I kiss your hips.
Then, mercifully, you bend your high brow,
allowing me to taste your angry lips.
And before I understand that this is dream,
I kneel to do what only I do best
in the valley where undying love was born.

Drowning Man

This afterlife seven fluorescent clouds
sail the still sky mirrored in his mind.
And for a moment he truly sees
the vision gasping beyond his prayer.

What multifarious light of dawn
as seagulls snatch and lift up his eyes
like hosts on the altar of the world
to the insouciance of the Lord.

What paradise of blinded kittens,
what heaven of flotsam washed ashore,
and Gabriel radiant in the sun
amid an army of idiots—

before the vision finally fades,
and the orgiastic birds let go
in the dark chambers of flooded lungs,
leagues, leagues—bright eternities below ...

Dylan Thomas

Although a sea of whisky filled each lung,
he would have called out from beneath a wave
just to console the living, but his tongue
was heavy as a stone inside the grave.

Eastertide

A sudden brightness. Call it day.
Rooks above the cathedral, and clouds
a thousand shades of morning grey,
while underneath: the coiling crowds
bear their pastries and precious fruit.
The cobble-stones shimmer in the rain
as "glory, glory" the bells bruit
past the sinners along the lane.

Eden

1) Adam

He'd pray if he knew how,
but his brain at this stage
can only concentrate
on simple survival. Now

is more important than
a blue-haired afterlife,
than a spiritual struggle
in which half-sentient men

must make a choice: between
a serpent and a god.
His cave has no bear skulls,
no finger-painted scene.

There is no chipped flint spear-
head on his wooden staff.
He knows this: hunger, lust,
rain, sunshine, snow and fear.

Himself prey amid the tall
trees of the primal forest,
he's innocent—untouched
by any imagined fall.

2) Eve

What was she then, using
her teeth to strip raw flesh
from the rib of an aurochs?
Was there any musing

in her fierce female eye,
or was there only want,
a brute babe in her womb,
the predator-filled sky

above her tangled hair?
Compelled to eat the fruit
hanging from the tree
nearby the serpent's lair,

she was shaped by a life
of stalking and devouring.
The hunter and the hunted,
she was Adam's wife.

3) Cain & Abel

Surely they were aware
of death; as boys the bones
of beasts were their most loved
possessions. They'd trap a hare

nearby its warren, bash its
skull against a rock, enjoy
the steaming brains,
warm on their tongues, then dash

back to the fire-lit cave
to help skin hides. A bear
skull would become all they
knew of deity, save

the roar of thunder, flash
of lightning. Adam, in his
nine-hundredth year, would offer
the bear skull ochre ash,

and yet it looked back coldly.
Only Abel could
appease the empty eyes
with rhino liver, boldly

going out each dawn
with a staff tipped with flint.
Cain with his wooden spear
began to wish him gone.

Never before had two men
killed for anything
but the flesh of beasts,
and the breasts of women.

Standing over the corpse
of his dead brother, Cain felt
relieved. The sky was silent;
a white cloud sailed on course.

Abel wouldn't be missed,
he thought. Both Eve and Adam
wept, and cursed the serpent,
though it had never hissed.

Epistle from the Dark

Lost in your catacombs, I've uncovered
the dank walls of effaced fishes. Branded
by the infidels above, I'll never
leave the ensconcing darkness. I'm stranded—

here, lukewarm and famishing for real food,
the kind that Origen, that eunuch, says
will hoist my shackled soul out of the brute
prison of my body. Here, dark are my days,

but what slight light there is, is oh so bright.
I've befriended forgotten patriarchs,
(those modest moles who've found peace in your night).
I've shed my last aesthetic tears and parts,

accepted the mercy of my sentence,
and would truly believe, in you, if not
for my ineffectual prayers. Silence
is all I hear, my fabulous dear God.

Eschatology

When the mind melts in the cave of the skull,
forsaken, alas, like everything else,
will some victorious Socrates crawl—
out of the depths, like a most secret self—

beholding all things as they really are?
Then, apostolic, but shunning the smell,
will he crawl back down inside—to pole-star
and enlighten the blind monkeys in hell?

Fettered to our forefathers' desires
and at odds with the light, no doubt those apes
won't listen, for madness never tires,
storming through our eyes and roping our napes.

And our magnanimous clear-sighted Greek,
that spark in the dung, our most secret self,
will he weather the worms of the first week,
forsaken, alas, like everything else?

Exile

He looks up at what pierces cloud,
but doesn't know it's epiphany—
this moment wind blows over sea
and dark's forgiven in its tracks.

He sees the field a boy once ploughed,
nostrils piqued by blossoming flax,
and thinks the questions no one asks,
eyes mirroring eternity.

Beyond the headland waves break loud.
Once again Boreas smacks
his pale and hypothermic lips.

Summer suddenly turns to Fall.
Behind him now the sunken ships
will never take him home at all.

Fly in Amber

At present there's a mall and a strip show.
Ronald McDonald waves to passing cars.
And yet a hundred million years ago
a forest stood beneath the same bright stars.
The Great Bear was still nameless in the sky.
There were no men to gaze up at the moon,
to hide in terror, holding back a cry.
In deep December it was sultry June.
The fly lay soused in sticky sap since dawn.
Yet thousands of millennia had fled
till it was picked up from the forest lawn.
A hapless hunter bartered it for bread.
Now a barfly pawns it for cold beer
and an æon seems but a single year.

For an Old Flame

Do you recall how I would buy champagne
with subway tokens at the Benson store,
then lick it all up from your northern breast?
        You still wore boots from Bialystok

and I would hold your bag in sun and rain.
Do you recall your mattress on the floor,
how we would suck and fuck and never rest,
        explore Manhattan, and then talk

our way down Clinton Street in funny rags?
It was four in the afternoon, my pocket
full of dreams you'd never tread on, love.
        I'd go back home, no longer vagrant,

listen to Cohen, look through plastic bags,
makeshift curtains, out at sunlight, locket
of your hair in my eyes, your smell above
        my grateful lips still warm and fragrant.

For Enoch Powell

The hooded hip-hop scum
heap up the funeral pyre;
the streets of London burn,
and yet, despite the fire,

the bobbies watch and turn
their visored faces away,
as if deaf, blind and dumb,
and England not lost its way.

Two thousand twelve has shown
that you are right again.
Forced to beg and undress,
still-lifed on a smart phone,

men bow and women bend
in multi-cultural fright.
Gone is the wilderness,
gone your voice in the night.

Frozen Stiff

To my enrainbowed eyes the trees are walking,
and the hawk is still as headland cliff.
What utter rapture at the end of stalking,
my dear Lord, now that I fly frozen stiff.

Each snowflake is a prism or a mirror
in a gallery of grimacing flame,
and every squealing self to You no dearer
than the birds that You hunt down for game.

You are, at last, a talon in the light
that clings in flight to a fear-stricken dove,
and I am the tears in the wake of fright
amid the falling feathers of our love.

Garbage

One rarely finds
just wholesome scraps:
a slice of ham,
potato rinds,
a glob of jam,
beer bottle caps.

Inside this drum
there's other stuff:
a blouse that's torn,
a hiker's thumb,
two clips of porn,
hardcore and snuff.

Godfather

He'll part this world with feathers on his feet,
the ton of five & dime cement no longer heavy,
his battered brow resembling morning wheat
as sunup blesses rusty Dodge and Chevy.

And hipsters coming out saloon and church
will mark a glimmer of unworldly light
when for a second he climbs walls to perch
by Jesus, having left for good the night.

And yet, his debt now paid in full, he'll bask
in glory on the surface of the sun
as bubbles rise and peel away his mask,
and he himself, no longer on the run,

embraces peace, peace that will greet us all
(the twin of silence in that timeless land),
since feathers and cement won't break our fall
and faith's too airy to provide a hand.

Grass

Before they built this mall and palace
I flourished longer than the clouds
remember; but it wasn't malice
caused me to be replaced by crowds.

I rise again in clear defiance,
Wait till the ordinance rescinds,
Spread into the cracks of silence,
blind seed scattered by the winds.

I hold out till the end of malls,
rise when the shopper ties his laces,
wait till the palace busts and falls.
Then I will cover names and faces.

Grey Oak

I turn the stony corner
where the graveyard begins.
Today I am a mourner.

Crows circle garbage bins
beyond the iron gate;
two magpies poach hairpins;

a sparrow comes too late,
then flees the treasure chest.
I move on, and I wait.

It is here she will rest
beneath the silt and sand,
her headstone facing west.

And still, I can't withstand
the power of my grief.
A tree can't understand
the falling of its leaf.

Had I Not Grown Suddenly Short of Breath

Had I not grown suddenly short of breath,
I'd have sung hosannas. But the poor beast
that I found lay martyred beyond its death.

The holy sun was rising in the East,
and I was watering bright illusions
as sweet and as old as Plato and Christ.

Birds in arbours were making allusions
to Eden, and I was bound for a tryst
with a seamstress, with Angel Jones of Mold.

But the writhing and the buzzing woke me
and the foul stink in the mystical gold,
for, breathless, I stopped and wept to behold,
as some dead poet's angry stick poked me,

a fawn in a laughing hyena's hold.

Hank

He finds himself alone again, pig-drunk
on the third planet from the sun, his thought
maudlin, stale as umpteen years ago,
but fresher than the whisky in his mouth.
Through failure he finds solace in the funk
of ten o'clock. The Nashville moon has not
yet touched him like the talons of a crow.
One with the evening, he will not fly south,
guitar strapped just behind the sprawling wings
of a misunderstood angel, cough and voice
inspired in the wake of careful choice.
He'll linger in the drawling words he sings,
the hero of this blue and lonesome story
while love moves on, and basks in all the glory.

Heraclitus

"a dry soul is wisest and best"

Biographers write that above all men
he was a lofty and hubristic spirit.
A walking contradiction, he would shout
that Homer should be turned out of the lists
and beaten, and Archilochus as well,
since better to extinguish impertinence,
than to put out fire. He felt that men
should fight for law as much as for their city.
Yet, when requested to make laws for them,
he turned them down, by arguing their city
already had a faulty constitution.
Besides, he had important things to do:
a game of dice with children at the Temple.
(It was there his magnum opus lay.)
Turned misanthrope, he headed for the hills
where for years he fed on grass and plants.
Only when afflicted with edema
would he come back down, asking the physicians
if they could bring drought after heavy rain.
When they said no, he smeared his trunk and face
with ox manure, and dried out in the sun.
He was discovered dead the following day,
his parched lips now two gates to the Sahara,
the river in his veins not quite the same.

Here, Under the Weight

Here, under the weight of an unknown sentence,
under the lead and the slate of the sky,
someone boozes and babbles to the silence,
but I'm not sure who, though together we die.

Here, under the weight of a sharpened axe,
under an executioner's tearless eye,
someone waits and prays and desperately asks
clinging faithfully to an age-old lie.

Here, under the weight of a knotted rope,
under the narrowing noose of his crime,
someone thinks and disbelieves, full of hope:
forever lasts only as long as time.

Hindenburgstraße 8

What German family must have once lived here?
Built in '32, the building's façade
was freshly made, the face of every god
and angel brand-new. Nowadays they sneer,

looking out sooty niches, ears and noses
riddled by history and acid rain.
Wort and stinkweed prosper where once roses
brushed against each crystal window pane.

The name is ul. Konarskiego now,
although the unkempt building still speaks German.
Inside the tenants' children do not ask how
as late at night the floorboards creak, and vermin

crawl the crevices and climb the walls.
The progeny of Slavs are not the same.
The ouster lasts, another system falls,
the vanquished having vanished with their name.

Hunter

Oh, but a thought ago a baying hound
had led him to a clearing in the sky.
The stars tolled beyond the sombre clouds
and on the frozen pond the forest sighed.

He knelt, his arrows whetted by a tear,
the fire he'd set, rising into night.
Eternity approached, and in its sphere,
a sudden passing bird eclipsed the light.

He aimed and freed an arrow into dark.
Then maelstroms, downy plumes, snow tainted red,
the pity of the moon: he hit his mark.

The hellward bird now tumbling overhead—
past hunger, fear, dumbfoundedness and shame—
an angel, angel falling into flame.

Invocation

Open the doors of the dark,
knock down the black spectres
that we might behold branches
ripe with dew.

We'll wet our cracked lips
with cool unworldly water,
and never cast a doubt
or curse the unminding moon.

Let the rutty road not burn,
a worm not canker our cores,
and wholehearted,
we'll follow like cherubim.

Let our brows' brine
not blind our vision,
the pain from our sores
not sully our spirits,

and we'll say
the world's not a whim
or a stupid tale
full of sound and fury.

Open the doors,
or desperately,
we'll break them down with our fists.

Slide us some sense,
some light
under the gates of worry.

Jacob's Ladder, 1888

The clouds are ragged as his clothes,
fox-grey and bloody from new wounds.
The river is a vein that flows
towards his hermit heart, festooned

with briars, and with poison oak.
Five beaver pelts press on his spine;
the spirit of an arrow strokes
his beard; his sweat turns into brine.

He'll build a tiny pillar of stone
in his mind, and only speak to those
who speak to him, for when alone
the Lord keeps him wherever he goes.

John Clare Escapes the Essex Asylum

How romantic they are in his mind,
crouched around the fire singing songs,
their sad emaciated dog behind
them, barking at the moon. He counts the wrongs,
pities them in his way, himself not right
in life, or ever in his troubled head.
He, too, beholds things in a different light.
Today the ale was malty, amber red,
yet like a grunting badger he now runs,
looking for Mary in the hazel woods.
He will not find her, or their ghostly sons.
He'll spend the night outside the Gypsy camp,
pipe in his mouth, bag full of stolen goods,
his mind warmed by sweet dreams, his body damp.

Journey Late at Night

My little boat unmoored,
I've drifted under stars,
but do not see the Lord,
just Artemis and Mars.

Above the deep, dark lake,
the moonlight's never said:
dawn is about to break
and heaven turn bright red.

Across the waves, an owl
has borne away its prey,
and something on the prowl
blasphemes the light of day.

The hope a mooncalf follows
is sacrifice for slaughter,
and yet the wings of swallows
still skip across the water.

Kant's Shadow

It stalked him to the end of fear,
like clockwork, down each Gothic street
of Königsberg, as if it knew
precisely when their hands would meet.

Last Poem

No new snow shrouds the ochre fields
on this the last December day.
Twelve months hence the last page yields,
and given up, your ghost turns grey.

Mist walking on the onyx river,
crows parting chalcedony clouds
embrace, forgive your heart or liver,
and bear your deeds into the wilds.

And now there's only purple flame,
grave moss that signifies release,
a poppy underneath your name,
or just a candle, spilt wax, peace.

Leaves

Leaves fall as if
from up the sky,
fall to form
their motley shrouds,

fall but never
question why,
amid the branches
and the clouds,

past the bramble
and the rose,
the sun above them
comes and goes,

but does not die.

Lermontov, Verlaine, Trakl, Yesenin . . .

A bullet buried deep inside his breast,
Lermontov lay dead, but forever young.
The Paris sun descending in the west,
Verlaine slept with green absinthe on his tongue.

The wounded soldiers in the Polish mud
stalked Trakl to the kingdom in his vein.
His final poem written down in blood,
Yesenin dangled by the window pane.

Four poets lived, then perished by default
by either pistol, bottle, drug or noose.
(It burns to write lines worthy of one's salt.)

And whether by God's grace, gift, guile, or ruse,
each climbed Parnassus as in an assault,
and sang with cup and chain until let loose.

Lobb Ghyll Viaduct

Behind thick bracken—I can almost see
an arch of millstone grit. Two small trains pass,
but only in the mind. Across the lea,
where sleepy heifers graze on Haw Pike's grass
or sprawl out underneath a buttermilk cloud,
I see the bluebells reaching up towards
damp haunches, ferns and forest garlic shroud-
ing steep wet banks, the flowers of ripe gourds.

I climb the summits of two Yorkshire hills
and see dismantled rails, the viaduct
buried by growth above a brook that rills,
dead as the ruins of Hag Head Laithe, tucked
far from the stacked-high cairn of Beamsley Beacon.
I see five dew-lit spans alive with lichen.

Ludwig Wittgenstein Visits Georg Trakl in Hospital, Cracow, 6 November 1914

"O stolzere Trauer! ihr ehernen Altäre,
Die heiße Flamme des Geistes nährt heute ein gewaltiger
Schmerz,
Die ungebornen Enkel."

The doves alight. The rooks cast shadows down.
And yet more trains arrive at Cracow Central
with wounded soldiers, while still others leave
for Görlitz and the not too distant front.
Ludwig Wittgenstein arrives with a frown,
his logical thoughts not yet transcendental,
his gold watch rubbing his grey jacket's sleeve.
He doesn't know yet what he will confront.
He doesn't know that he is three days late.
He doesn't know that Trakl lies cold and dead.
He'll take a tram and then walk down a lane.
He'll put his fingers on a rusty gate,
hear howls, smell wounds, behold a sky that's red.
And for the first time he will fathom pain.

Manichaeans

Indistinguishable from the dark, a rat
crawls through debris. Above, aloof and pale,
the moon shines on all the heavens and hells
of the city, shines on the good and bad

alike, more intimately than the sun.
Two pounds of dung sit in our bodies' bowels,
waiting to be released. The sweat on our brows,
the warm saliva on our twisted tongues

shall be purified in estuaries,
merge with the thoughts of seals and otters.
Our sperm and eggs become sons and daughters,
but what of the husks of all our worries,

of our falling lungs and aching gallstones,
of the scabs from our wounds, of our bad blood?
We prefer abstractions, words like: love
and redemption; hate the meat on our bones,

gag at the worms that cleanse us, yield to blight.
We are purists at heart. But, if only
it would stop pounding, if only we could be
fleshless, if only we could be like light.

Market

We went down to the market.
Your hand inside my pocket
was soft and ivory white,
your eyes two jewels bright
beneath gold locks of hair,
flowers in April air.

We walked where loving led,
and did not look ahead.
We did not see the hens
headless on the fence,
the quartered hogs on hooks,
the butcher's angry looks,

the crones with wizened hands
behind the tulip stands,
their thin grey hair unmade,
their eyes lit dim from trade,
devoid of beauty's powers,
but selling the same flowers.

Mary

When he beheld stars in her eyes at play,
and when he heard their laughter in her voice,
he never doubted. He could but rejoice:
Her soul was real, real as the Milky Way.

He was a planet spinning round her glow,
he was alive because she was the sun.
But that was when their marriage had begun,
so many warm, bright memories ago.

These nights she sits inside the winter house,
her hands limp in a flowered kiddy-bowl,
her supper splattered on her bib and blouse,

her eyes, her eyes—now denser than a hole
that over pink horizons of their scars—
blackens planets and eclipses stars.

Mary Magdalene

When Mary washed his feet he didn't stare
down like an ordinary man. No lust
blazed in his eyes, although her milky bust,
thighs and neck were there for him. Her hair
brushed his calves, her hands reached past his knees.
She was just doing what she'd always done.
It was still early. Her lips had just begun.
Her earthly thoughts commingled with the breeze.
He focused on what was to come: his trial,
his torture and his death. He didn't want it,
rebuking Mary with a gentle smile.
She covered up with sorrow and a veil.
And I sign my name beneath this sonnet,
a man who lusted and who knew her well.

Metaphysics

This is the last goodbye, the final salute.
From beneath the cover of a flag
the ensign is assisted down the chute
so neither flank nor limb can catch a snag.

Then at last his sunken eyes see light,
And he sets foot into the promised land.
Effulgent plankton there redeems his sight,
Elysium of bright seaweed and sand.

How glorious his underwater grave,
even though above, the stone-faced captain
sees a guilty spectre in each wave,
and dejection overwhelms the chaplain.

And the crew? They're busy swatting flies,
the smoke from guns still burning in their eyes.

Migrations

Through bleary eyes I hear migrating birds
at morning. Over meadows, down into
the valley of my ears, they follow words
whispered in dreams. And only for this do

I keep faith in the alchemy of rays.
They will return when ice breaks in the river,
when my mind sinks in the mud of May's
tadpole-like embryo, flock to deliver

their paeans over my salt and pepper hair
as I rise from the shadow of their wings,
my thoughts entangled in a spider's lair,
groping to overhear a bell that rings.

Moonshine, 1969

Grandpa had a gambler's poker face,
though grandma held the tattered deck of cards.
We crossed the bridge in Wheatland, and then raced
by Dunbar Slag, and two scrap metal yards.
Old Bill was sleeping near his pit-bull Pug,
but woke when he caught ear of grandpa's voice.
They went inside, then came out with a jug
of what Old Bill called "Pennsylvania's Choice."
They drank it like spring water, cold and pure,
reminisced about what two old fogies
had done for cash in nineteen twenty-four,
then grandpa smiled and said: "We'd better go."
Before we got back home he smoked two stogies,
stinky ones, so grandma wouldn't know.

Moose

A little slow and thick around the waist,
she was fond of wading in the muck.
Always late, she would walk into class,
then take her place behind a nerd or geek.
Freckled and blonde, and masculine of shoulder,
she looked like Butkus ready for the grid,
and yet her soft blue eyes betrayed a dancer,
the Isadora Duncan of tenth grade.
I was the quiet boy who sat up front,
who weighed his words and loathed all cruelty,
and yet one day I spoke and made her hurt.
The name I gave her chased her through the hallway,
followed her home, and everywhere she moved,
down the decades and into the grave.

Mother in the Garden

Mother tends the blooms as she has done
for as long as I am able to recall.
She stands, supported by prosthetic knees,
the heat of August heavy on her brow.
I want to call her in, afraid the sun
will cause a stroke. I think of last year's fall,
how she lost her balance trimming trees.
I try to call her in, but by a row
of roses, she cannot quite hear or see.
I hurry down the potted back porch stairs,
past the plum-stained bench and phlox-filled tins.
Transfixed, one foot into eternity,
one foot upon the earth, she turns and grins,
her blue eyes brilliant and beyond my cares.

Obituary

Today I leaf through the obituaries
and find out who has died among the famous—
an actress, doctor, and philanthropist—
the stories of their lives take up a page.

But I recall my neighbour, Betty Amos,
who, with beads wrapped round a gnarled fist,
attempted to cure cancer with Hail Marys,
never letting faith succumb to rage.

There is no mention of her name at all,
no words relating kindnesses and deeds,
how she brought us apples in the fall,
and fed the hungry pigeons pumpkin seeds.

Old Generals

When you are an old general, you know you're going to go anyway.

You lead for your people & for your men, whom you not only want to win, but to survive the battle & the war.

To do this you will be hated, ostracized, & sacked in the end, but you will have won the war & saved your men.

Old Meerschaum Pipe

A friend sent a pipe made
from petrified sea foam,
froth that was life's first home.
A bearded craftsman's blade

carved it into the face
of man: the progeny
of an amoeba, the
image of his race.

It sits for all to see,
like a bust on the shelf:
in-cognizant of self,
yet part of the same sea,

its beauty and its scars,
its yellow stain and reek,
the wrinkle on its cheek:
the stuff of dreams and stars.

Old Tarts

They come at eight o'clock
and never are they late
for the church bell to toll
over the iron gate.

Above their heads a school
of ravens haunts the skies.
A priest unbolts the lock;
dew gathers in their eyes.

Arthritic, gnarled, and bent,
their brittle aching bones
creak like old bordellos
a pimping cocksman owns.

They pray for their bedfellows
and cling to rosaries.
Piously they keep Lent
and wait for their release.

Onion Snow

The peeps you'd bought were chirping in the box.
The groundhog lied again. You'd left to buy
beer, bread and chipped ham. It was Easter Sunday.
Bells from a dozen churches filled the air
in this small steel town where the unemployed
perpetually keep beer gardens open.
You'd yelled: 'Yunz better worsh them dishes
and redd up things before yunz go outside.'
You said you'd had enough of eating jumbo
and food stamps didn't make a difference.
We didn't know you'd go by way of Altoona,
that you'd go ghost on mommy and us kids.
You left behind a bloodstain in your truck,
the lasting memory of onion snow.

On the Beheading of Lee Rigby

It's true: few deaths are kind.
The agéd pensioner,
with Dunkirk on his mind,
prays for his to occur.

His life was long and hard;
a belt still burns his back.
Inside the cancer ward
he lies upon the rack.

To die at ninety-five
is not a tragedy.
To part a hornet hive
is to die peacefully.

To be killed in one's prime,
run over in the street,
is an unspeakable crime
no one should ever meet.

In Britain's largest city
a soldier returning to base,
young fusilier Lee Rigby,
was slain because of race.

In the name of belief
because Albion fights
its Wars for Tel Aviv
to uphold human rights?

Whose? Certainly not Lee's
who lay upon the pavement
that every white man sees.
There freedom means enslavement.

Out Back

Amid the sudden flurries, shrill
bells toll beneath December cloud.
Martha opens lids, her will
one with the rooks that curse out loud:
another day on bitter earth
passes over Tinker Hill.

Reeking of mackerel culled from tins,
she bends for something of true worth,
reaches into a toppled barrel
the moment a miracle begins,
and, off-key, sings a Christmas carol
to celebrate a kitten's birth.

Out On Your Feet

You have just taken the umpteenth blow
to whatever cheekbones you have left.

Your nose now is an orphaned limb
that hangs from bloody snot and gristle.

Your teeth are shards of broken glass
between the ridges of your gums.

Your mind is pig-shit, scrambled eggs,
and your thoughts are the intervals

in the longest count since Dempsey
stood over Tunney in Soldier Field.

And yet you still stand there and smile
at the birth and death of sudden stars,

an afterlife so imminent,
hoping the ref won't stop the fight.

Papa's Dying

Visionary underneath his pain,
he lies there, staring blankly at my mother,
cancer spread from his liver to his brain.
She tries to tell him all the latest news,
mentions I'm in flight, and that my brother
and sisters are beside his bed. They smother
him with their grief. My brother offers booze.
But papa calls out to his long-dead father,
points to his own bare feet with his cane,
and asks them to take off his heavy shoes.

Passenger Pigeons

I'd lift my forehead from the book and see
a flock consisting of a billion birds,
like a river in the heavens, three
miles wide, and forty miles in length. My words
never pierced the shadow they cast down.
Born more than eighty years too late, I could
not warn them of the threat of each new town,
of hunters waiting in the underwood.
For hours they were sovereigns to my eyes,
passing over Mercer County. The sun
gilded their feathers in the bloody twilight,
and when they vanished over the horizon
towards Ohio, Michigan, and the night,
what I heard were not coos, only cries.

Philosopher

For a moment as brief and long as eternity
he sees what the blind man sees in the blink of an eye:
a sun that never sets, forms wrought from gold, purity
before it falls or is restored to grace, the grey sky

beheld from the far side of dawn. As if in a dream,
he walks amid universals, essences of names,
and marvels at the beauty of birds, the snowflakes teem-
ing through the ethereal windows of souls, and the flames

of dear dead Heraclitus—now at last understood.
For as long as a moment *is* he sees the Father
embrace the Son—forever since the onset of time.

He has climbed out of the phantasmical cave for good,
martyred by what rills in the blood, no longer bothered
by those in fetters—yet part of the natural crime.

Pilitak

The agéd Eskimo, once *sangilak,*
the strongest of them all, prepares to die.
Today he will not shield a slanted eye,
nor starving in the evening stagger back.

Having fought a bear and years of cold,
fresh salmon never leave his fingertips,
and caribou blood never parts his lips.
And yet, he's lost his balance and his hold.

He's *pilitak,* of help, but little use.
So he lies on a bed of tundra ice,
awaiting *kadzait,* wandering wolves, his eyes
blind in the twilight like those of a moose.

Slow, pleasant, death will come at six or seven
in the wake of a fierce blizzard storm,
(hypothermia and crystal form),
and it will be all he will know of heaven.

Plato Returns to Earth

In the utter clarity of that new dawn,
having wrestled Socrates all night
until a world of purest forms was drawn,
he put away his thoughts and stepped outside,
and saw a new sun on the far horizon,
felt a cool breeze lifted from the sea,
then heard a flock of gulls philosophizing
on what lasts longer than philosophy.

Poem in October

On this breezy October morn, I walk
in the swift shadows of cloud-cursing rooks,
watching the world wake on the horizon.

In the brush I hear the tangerine talk
of blackbirds, and, in a crumbling wall's nooks,
the tumult of thrushes halving a bun.

And I see the first cart of dawn turning
the corner, see its owner's toothless grin
amid a pile of leaves lit by the sun.

And I smell the scent of something burning,
of something smouldering deep within,
fouler than all the hills of Polish dung.

Thirty-five years have transformed my life's leaves
into an outcast's smoke upon the breeze.

Poor Man's Diamond

I'd go out, see Agnieszka behind
the splintered greyness of the wind,
red maple leaves so close I'd touch
them in their resurrected flights.

I'd lug a hard-on in my pocket,
or chunk of looking-glass bright coal,
pretend it was a genuine diamond
and offer it on a dime-store string.

Love had turned me into alchemist.
But a woman with ambition,
she gave it back to keep me warm,

heat from her fingers like a furnace
twenty calendar years later
whenever I shave or comb grey.

Praised Be

Praised be the ugly and the beautiful,
the slow decay of leaves, the dew on grass,
the thistles and the apples bountiful.
Praised be the frozen branches in the pass,
the rapids rushing downwards to the spring,
the violets sprouting in the morning light.
Praised be the feather of the broken wing,
the wounded fawn that will not last the night
whose heavy clouds obstruct the moon and stars.
Praised be the hungry lynx and its last prey,
the goshawk flying over woodland scars
before it dives into a sea of grey.
Praised be the fierce light that forever burns,
and life that struggles, dies and then returns.

Puddle

Under swooning clouds
you look into the gleam
of a puddle after rain.
And, as if in a dream,

you see yourself reflected
in the wavelets, wind
blowing locks of hair
as you reach down, though pinned

yourself against the bottom,
which is heaven or hell,
depending on your point
of view, or just a well.

Quasimodo

As he lies mid his retinue of rats,
oblivious to the trickling water
and the maelstrom in the babbling sewer,
one might think his nose a hovel for flies
in the low and oppressive August heat,
but gladly he sleeps the sleep of the just,
like a foetus double-crossed in the womb.

Who but the passing ethereal white clouds,
or the bent proprietress of a dive
in those drunken days before her passing,
ever noticed to care by whim or chance
how he resembled a pigeon walking
in the ocean of misery and mud
neighbouring the cathedral of the damned?

Or how he spit when he spoke over bowls
of steaming porridge in the good hospice
run by six eternally stoned eunuchs,
his words brilliant as moonshine through stained glass,
simple as the stars in their begging truth,
though none and all understood their meanings
by the soft intonations of his grunts?

And now for the umpteenth and final time
he lies high in a heap like a dunghill
waiting for the street-cleaners to clean him up,
the sun bursting through his shuttered eyelids,
his eardrums full of Gregorian chants,
while the rats scurry like flawed apostles
in the wake of flapping but broken wings . . .

Racked Beauty

Blest be the dawn, the luminous blue-slate,
the arch transfused by the glorious sun,
and blackbirds chanting hymnals in prickly bushes,
and rooks high over fields coughing up love.

Blest be the winds about the furrowed brow,
and the joyful whispers of dying leaves,
the maples staggered blissfully behind barbed fences
above the tombs of the newly redeemed.

Blest be pain that comes like a stark beggar,
the thorn-tree that has its roots in a star,
the sweet massacred gourds tethered to the rusting gate,
the apples heaped on the agonized floor.

Raggedy Anne

Through woollen tresses of her limp red hair,
will she conjure ghosts to pry the locks? —
He wonders as he climbs the creaking stair
to lay her in an attic storage box.

Enchanted is the freckled face she wears
these days so darkened by his daughter's death.
She is too daft and fey to grasp his cares—
down the seven years of fostered breath.

Her eyes are brilliant as the breaking dawn
afire with the news of Eastertide,
as if faith could bring back the dead and gone,
or put a rib back into Adam's side.

May she see endless mercy grant a pardon
to her elder sister struck at play.
And may she see pure light in Eden's garden
though he himself sees only dark through grey.

Reunion

It will be such and such a year,
the sun appearing now and then,
clouds over cola, booze and beer,
teenagers now grey-bearded men,
corn on the cob and sizzling meats,
smoke from a charcoal-heated grill.
There will be women, cries, and feats,
dandelions on a hill,
twister, spin the bottle, hide
and seek. There will be joy and laughter,
marshmallows, bonfire and hayride,
a game of softball the day after.
Only you will lag behind,
Nineteen Eighty-Four no nearer—
your clothing, hairstyle, language, mind—
trapped inside a rear-view mirror.

Rust Belt

You turn your thoughts away from your own yard,
grandchildren skipping rope and tossing balls.
The bell rings and you're running down the halls
of the old school past frog-faced Mrs. Sward
until you reach a desk, a wobbly one
with "Johnny loves Annette" engraved on it.
You look out of the window at the lit
blast furnaces, the molten morning sun
that was your immigrant pop's bread and butter.
His heavy accent lingers in your mind,
his calloused fingers tousling teenage hair.
A while ago you left him in the stutter
of half goodbye. And now you look behind
inside a school that is no longer there.

Saint Francis of Ninth Avenue

Coughing, he unlocks the iron-clad door,
and a flock of gold and silver keys
rises like an inverted pyramid
over his little kitchen for the poor.

The gnarly, the disabled, weak of knees,
the drunk, the ugly, stoned and plain stupid
stand in the shit and shadows of his doves,
sobered by the wrath of a cold breeze.

Squinty-eyed himself, he is not blind
to avarice, nor to their push-and-shoves.
Holding a pipe in his yellow hand,
he touches with the fingers of his mind,
and watches those not even morning loves
enter and re-enter the promised land.

Saturday Market

Jabka, apples, *slivki*, plums.
She points to fruit with her gnarled hand.
He smiles and tries to understand,
fondling with fingers and with thumbs.
Nearby, another vendor hums
a song from some exotic land,
a land of coffee, dates and sand.
Another opens pickle drums,
hangs a chain of smoked frankfurters.
Another grins, displaying leek
& morel cheese.
        Though there are fences,
here mid the chimes of dimes and quarters,
people smile to say they speak
the Esperanto of the senses.

Satyr

Waiting for our turns at Louie the Barber's,
we look through porn culled from the coffee table,
at the silicon breasts, the buck-green eyes,
and listen to the dirty jokes, each fable

of conquest. A draft from a swirling fan
spreads the scent of booze and talcum powder.
And we avert our eyes from the long face,
the ugly young man in the chair, as louder

the clippers buzz, and locks of golden hair
fall from his scalp, commingling with the dust.
Goat-like, with pimples oozing pus and blood,
he evokes not pity, but disgust:

the thought that we too must sit in the chair,
we with our porn, our dirty jokes, our folly,
the booze in our guts like gehenna's flames,
but all of us still beautiful and holy.

.

Saviour

How well he knew the wives of publicans,
come-hither smiles beneath the crumbling arches,
the lingering scent of unattended cunts.
He too was half mad, fond of *garum*, March's
sombre unforgiving leaden sky.
Yes, he paid taxes, cursing Midas most.
Like all false prophets he was wont to lie,
the wine upon his tongue his holy ghost.
So when they nailed him to a wooden cross,
two centuries before Lord Jesus Christ,
he did not shout in anger at his father.
He sailed amid the midnight sky, across
the Milky Way—foot, finger, hand and wrist
prostrate—till he himself could go no farther.

Silesian Landscape

The January wind
Bangs
against the window-panes,

maliciously twists
the black bones
of shivering trees,

racks
Baroque clouds
in a scudding cycle
of dreams,

under which rooks,
like cast-out
angels,

frolic,
cough up hermetic
blasphemies

on a grey day
without snow.

St. Martin's Cemetery

(New Derry, Westmoreland County, PA)

Grandfather Lawrence, whom I never knew,
I wonder what appeasing light, if any,
may have eased your pain and strengthened you
as blind and bleeding underneath the many
winding caverns of the hellish earth,
your starved lungs gasping for a final breath,
you prayed for some miraculous rebirth
to justify the agony of death.

But what your friends could rescue from the ground
resembled only contours of a man.
And none dared utter words or make a sound
when Hilda (mother of my mother) ran
and tried to recognize your blackened face,
then covered it with light from her embrace.

Stone

Only this stone is certain,
if only for a moment.
I touch it and look down
at the dark sea, a curtain

behind which life here started,
reminded that all things
are in a state of flux,
the living and departed.

And yet the bell still rings
over the sun-lit hill.
A padre gives a sermon
about eternal things.

"The Father sacrifices
his one and only Son."
The fruit of an amoeba,
morphed into man, devises

an escape, the burden
too difficult to bear?
If only for a moment
only this stone is certain.

Storks in August

Over the birches and into the sun
sail the storks southwards to Africa,

from the rooftops of pale northern farmers,
to the grazing fields of Zulu herdsmen.

The weakest will expire along the way
before they cross the straits of Bosporus,

others be poached, or trapped in power lines,
felled over olive groves in the Levant.

At winter's close the strongest will return,
some wounded but miraculously living

with arrowheads protruding from their necks
or birdshot lodged in their majestic wings,

to build their nests in European hamlets,
on chimneys and the roofs of nursery schools.

Over the birches and into the sun
sail the storks southwards to Africa.

Sufi

*"Mansur Al-Hallaj, having heard of
Christ the martyr, came to Baghdad
whirling on his feet, and forgave the
Caliph and his officials even before they
did anything to him."*

Yet for this kind of love they chopped
his left foot off and broke his leg,
for knowledge such as this they lopped
his right hand off, and left a peg
of shattered bone to greet the ghost
of martyrdom inside his prayer,
then pinned him bat-like to a post,
inverted, so his scrotum, bare
to all, hung over his limp prick, within
the gloom and glow of light, before
they poked him with their stick on
what was his last living night.
And then they gathered round like curs
as he whirled through the universe.

Summit

The summit is the goal, although the way
is thorny and rough. The bark of spruces brushes
your arms as you await the sudden ray,
and beetles pock your skin as water rushes

in the stream beneath the rocky ridge.
It's taken you a half a century
to get this far. Below the hanging bridge,
there is a skeleton and broken knee,

soiled jeans, torn shirt, boots caked with clay and mud,
a little temple, and what looks like a scar.
Yet biding your time was enough, the thud

of your heart now the echo in dry blood, lips
watered by the moon and the first star
weeks after the drought following the flood.

Swallows

It was once thought that swallows
wintered on the moon,
or morphed into field mice
beneath the autumn swoon

of clouds, or slept beneath
wavelets on the floor
of shadowy ponds and lakes
until the sudden lure

of springtime roused them from
the kingdom of the dead.
Early Christians believed
they swirled around the head

of Jesus, giving comfort
as he bore his heavy cross,
or they were harbingers
of heaven after loss.

Today I look above
the eaves as autumn blooms
in the deep well of the sky,
my house's empty rooms

echoing only wind,
the memory of their song.
They have flown south for winter,
which here is dark and long.

Swamp

There is more here than mist,
duckweed and spatterdocks.
A bowfin, three-feet long,
lurks amid the stalks

of cattails, preying on
a school of yellow bass.
A pickerel prowls amid brown
tamaracks and grass.

A snapper with musket shot
still lodged inside its tail,
devours a bloated frog,
exposing only its shell.

And at the water's edge,
a towering black gum,
old as the Liberty Bell,
watches deaf and dumb.

Its leaves soon will turn red
for the three hundredth autumn:
a leaf for every brave
buried at the bottom.

Tattie Bogel

His world is ochre over which a crow
at dusk flies home. A bankrupt's house and barn,
a field assailed by January snow,
the river winding like a spinning yarn.

No human drama in his straw-filled frame,
as he hangs, facing nature hard at work:
the lynx in the black thicket hunting game,
the maelstrom in the icy water's murk.

No father comes down from a sunlit cloud to
save the lemmings headed for the shore.
There is the smell of raw meat, blood and bone,

deer fur spewed under oak trees in the wild.
There is no Pilate, Lazarus, or poor.
And yet the cross is heavier than stone.

Tesla, 1939

The winos on the benches, in between
swigs and catnaps, would refer to him
as Saint Francis of Bryant Park. It was

he who fed pigeons, from compassion or
compulsion? Alternating current had,
no doubt, already touched his brilliant mind.

The father of the wireless connection,
he'd reach into his bag, half-idiot,
half-genius, whispering in tender coos.

Having towered over both Marconi
and Edison, he'd toss the creatures crumbs
as part of some hermetic ritual.

Then he'd hightail it back to his small room,
converted years before into a roost,
and wait for his true love, a white dove.

He'd brood beside her on the *Teleforce*,
a weapon to end all wars. And when she died
he understood his work on earth was done.

The Adolf Hitler Canal

Look from the bridge down into the black waters
where, corroded, rest the sunken barges.
A riddled sapper never set the charges:
the cry of birches is a wife's or daughter's.

Ilya Ehrenburg had opened the locks
in January nineteen-forty-five.
Mute as the dead are the raped left alive.
Now only splendid architecture talks.

The skeletons of quays rust in the spring,
their wooden floor beds long since warped and rotten.
Thorn and thistle prosper on the shore.

The opening ceremony with Hess forgotten,
the hammer and the sickle crush and sting
like history writ by those who won the war.

The Barn

Thinking far back, looking through the wild
late summer weeds, the thorny brush, you see
tar paper hanging from its roof, loft piled
with bales of sweet but rotting timothy.

You see its termite-eaten stanchions, beams
exposed, as coal-black voles traverse its gut.
You see the purple farmer lost in dreams,
unmortgaged, who will never witness what

misfortune has befallen him. You see
the knotted rope, the morning moving about,
following the bailiff's narrow shadow. You see
the sudden ray. You wonder and you doubt.

The Bell

You hear the bell, the sun upon your shoulders
like a spilt bag of gold, the street awash
with piss and lager as the hated soldiers

of the sewers dodge the morning's shrapnel,
shrewd in their retreats beneath the lash
of a self-righteous eye, although a capful

of coins collected on the narrow street
could never alter them from being what
they are: roof rats escaping with the wheat

of an old flour mill, while a fly-clad baker
hangs suspended from beams, as if caught
by Peter at the foothill of the gate.

You hear the bell, and walk towards your maker,
sun on your shoulders, feet upon the grate.

The Birdman

"In Brueghel's Icarus, for instance: how everything turns away
Quite leisurely from the disaster..."
—W. H. Auden, from *Musée des Beaux Arts*

He rose to the caws of housewives, the joy
of rooks. And before he could unglue his eyes,
he whistled a prayer to the cold grey wind,
high on years of scrumptious insanity.
The Bagman in the gutter, the Hunchback
on the bench, the Scarecrow under the news,
watched him take off through the willows,
past Jack and the Beanstalk and Mother Goose.

Flapping his wings at the jackdaws, quacking
at the swifts, laughing at the landlocked joggers,
he soared beneath the bright hypocrisies
of a cloud towards the vagaries of God
in the vicinity of the blocked out sun,
but the ants below mistook his cries for dance
and his wingéd tears for a bucket of rain
amid a gehenna of swept up debris.

No sun had cast him down with melting wings
as he dove towards the duckweed in the pond,
watching the little sailing ships depart.
And only the Bagman in the gutter,
the Hunchback on the bench, the Scarecrow
under the news—saw Poseidon hug him
amid bubbles and ambiguous foam
in a heaven that does not mock our tears.

The Birdman of Gdansk

When cathedral bells toll through the morning
and sunlight touches steeples with its glare,
and arrows on the town hall clock stop turning,
you will find him on the market square,
sweeping leaves in shadows of despair.
And in that instant you will cease your yearning.
Hunchbacked, with a chuckle he will share
the secrets of his heart, and give a warning
to city doves assembling at his feet,
to sparrows quarrelling on Neptune's head.
He'll lower his tobacco chin to meet
their eyes and whisper what Saint Francis said.
He'll toss crumbs with his withered sailor's hand.
And when he looks up, you will understand.

The Bridge

Petalled with rust beneath a sky of slag,
the bridge expands into infinite haze.
Below it, the meaning of all my days:
thistled lots, brambled voids where time lags

oblivious to the maimed and forgotten.
My eyes sink in their vision: flocks of crows,
torrents of black water, flapping shadows
over tawny fields in endless autumn . . .

On the bridge, wasting bad time, I'd shed tears,
but have no regrets, only old ironies,
black insect prayers that cannot break my fall.

I'd appeal my sentence, seek solace from seers,
but the child in me knows: beyond destinies
light is everywhere, and redeems us all.

The Cat

I'd pass it on the mission trail—
   half-decomposed, green burr-like eyes
beyond my thoughts or pity, tail
   curled into questions only flies
would answer, as they staked their claim
   to rotting tissue. Food for worms,
and mocked by summer's honey flame,
   it had no choice but come to terms
with piecemeal dissolution. Those
   loud buzzes echoed in my ears
until it circled and then rose,
   converting me—some thirty years
since—into the lone passerby
   and witness, ever on my way
from daily service, like the sky
   itself on resurrection day.

The Careful Gardener

The garden has been left unkempt. Now thorn
and thistle thrive, burr, bramble and stinkweed.
The path that led to tulips, once well-worn,
is overgrown with wort and crabgrass seed.

What grand and stately gardens—Egypt, Greece
and Rome, though under the same sun and clouds
they perished. When great civilizations cease
existing their bleak ruins are but shrouds.

Thus we await the gardener's return,
who careful, dedicated to his work,
makes certain the weeds, pulled and gathered, burn
efficiently, since others loom and lurk.

Cheat brome and hemlock plot behind the scenes
to overtake the garden and the path.
For him it's not a war against bad genes,
but of survival, husbandry and math.

The Exit

The heart would heal, blood not sour in the veins,
the philosopher's cave not dim in the skull,
the body rise, and in the light, forget its pains,
the once mad apes freed by the glorious wall.

And all would climb the miraculous ladder,
eyes burning, behind mirrors, and in the sun:
see Your face, ineffable, but much sadder,
wrestling with what God for whose will to be done?

The Familiar Night

You leave the dive, the din behind the doors
forever shut. You stagger in the light
and watch rats bear the moon and stars away
into an afterlife of steaming sewers.
Face baptized by the quiet, hell to pay:
there's only you now, the familiar night.

The Garrett Loft

In garret lofts poor artists have quite often
painted women bathing, combing hair
inside a nearby mirror . . .
                                    Your eyes soften,
and, pale as blossoms or flesh from a pear,
your skin glints in the light. Snow falls outside
amid the greyness and the winter cold,
yet this one moment it is warm inside.

Crouched in the slipper tub, you sit and hold
your sprawling hair in your right hand, and comb
it with your left. You smile, sing to yourself,
and in the glass see pennies on the shelf,
a garret loft too bare to be your home.
And I see what those starving artists see
and try to catch it for eternity.

The Gathering Storm

The leaden marrow shrouds some brighter source.
Its boundaries are jaggéd and fluorescent:
a god's seaming white schizophrenic shores.

Beyond: is the blue of the firmament
and, perhaps, *Deitas*, the knowledge of—
glanced in a piercing flash, (even though pent
in the dark heavy flesh, under dandruff,
mucous, urine, and blood, the shackled soul
questions if its existence is enough
to win over the maggot in its stool).

And beyond that blue: it's blacker than bright:
the stars shine according to their own due.
And there at the edge: it's brighter than night
for the unworldly few.

The Idiot

Whenever I sit with the village idiot,
it's always with genuine reverence and a bit
of suspicion. Usually we just stare at the rooks,
and he sips my beer without asking, then looks
deranged as if to say he's sorry. He knows enough
about me to know I like diamonds in the rough.
And, strangely, he and I always notice the same things:
hieroglyphs in the snow, tiny holes in our fillings.
When he's not around, my wife says he's a blackguard
and a parasite, a charlatan, and a drunkard;
and I try to explain that he's just the village idiot, and
that once in a while it's necessary to sit
with him and share a pint. Later, when she falls asleep,
out of pity and out of love, I allow him to sneak
into her bed and fondle her thin white thighs,
and, if she doesn't protest, to spend the night.

The Moth

Although they've much in common: fear of night,
fear of the hour-glass's falling sands,
he traps a fleeting moth inside his hands
as it departs the darkness for the light.

It beats its wings in an impassioned fight
to force its way out, willfully demands
its freedom. But the power that commands
his own will—is unmindful of its plight.

He holds it fast, as if intent to show
that all depends upon the power's whim,
that if he dares to squeeze, or lets it go,
no wrathful god will judge or punish him.

Yet when his hands unfold, his conscience stings:
the powdery, white flakes—were once its wings.

The Obscure One

Left them far behind, their whetted spears
and painted faces, their bone-punctured noses,
but not as shaman or kahuna man—
as Heraclitus of south Borneo.

Lived alone for over twenty years
upon Mount Kinabalu, tending roses,
eating only grass and bamboo plant,
watching the Liwagu River flow.

Would not step into its waters twice.
Content to live far from humanity.
Began to crawl and talk to fleas and lice.
Befriended by a certain exotic bird.
Only it can see through obscurity,
        he thought, and understand his word.

The Poems

From nothingness the poems came to me,
warm and sensual as cats, their claws
digging deep into my ageing shins.
But when I looked into their bright green eyes,
they told me that they had no remedy
for madness or approaching death. Their paws
rest upon my lap now, and their chins
press soothingly against my mortal thighs,
as if to say that when I don't know how
to cope, disgusted by my life's deceit,
and forgetfulness has committed theft,
touching the many wrinkles on my brow,
they will be here to soften the defeat,
reminding me they're all that I have left.

The Scarecrow

Drunk on clouds and yesterday's rain,
his hollow eyes would hate the stars
and his hat shelter him from pain
to the whirr of distant passing cars,

but the cosmos inside his head
is only a vacuum of air:
he cannot feel my angst or dread,
though oft I think he knows despair.

Fastened to the stick of a broom,
his cramped straw feet would touch the ground
and his racked arms embrace the gloom
of anguished nights wound round and round,

but he won't tame a feral crowd,
nor build temples of a new faith,
nor in tears cry to God out loud,
nor enter heaven like a wraith.

Underneath an unminding moon
amid corn that spreads on and on,
he never lives and dies too soon
as endlessly, I wait for dawn.

The Snowman

"The Emperor of the Universe of pain
jutted his upper chest above the ice . . ."
—Dante Alighieri, *The Inferno*

Who fashioned him with burning hands of ice?
Who chiselled him out of the roofs of hell?
And for what purpose and what price
in the blind black eye of what winter gale?

Who lodged this parsnip deep into his brain?
Who placed this foolish crown upon his head?
And to whose profit and whose gain
in the wake of what wonder and what dread?

Who made him lord of his forsaken stare?
Who left him in this world of raspy cries?
And unto whose will and whose care
in the long shadow of such sad, cold skies?

The World to Come

There is a glimmer of the world to come in the ease
of the eyes of the homeless woman decked out in rags,
and there's a hint of glory in the castaway leaves
lying low in the gutters amid smouldering fags.

For I've seen Christs climb out of the flames of icicles
clinging to the rusty pipes where the forsaken dwell,
and I've seen the saved herded in suits before steeples
delighting in daybreaks indistinguishable from hell.

This Morning

for Dylan Thomas

This morning I woke to the sound of bells
and to the dark sermons of black-frocked rooks.
The air was fraught with the breaths of angels
and the sky stood strangely above the roofs.

This morning I woke with the taste of stale
liquor lingering on my twisted tongue,
and entered the deep grey of my heaven-hell
with a cirrhotic liver and mucous lung.

This morning I woke to the coughs of cars, to
the clangour of crammed trams turning
corners, kissing the whey-faced hush of a nun.

This morning I woke opening strange doors.
In the skull's temple: white candles were burning,
and the coins on my eyelids saw the same sun.

Transcendence

At dawn when sunlight penetrates the mist
and two or three migrating rooks curse heaven,
you hear church bells ring; at half past seven
see a drunkard rise and clench his fist.

Dark is the doorway you must enter. Smell
of mortal piss and shit. A garbage bin
teaming with Norway rats. You knock and tell
the bent custodian to let you in.

A shadow falls as from a movie reel
past potted plastic flowers lined in rows.
You can hear Mozart in the courtyard, feel
the bite of Hades in your blistered toes.

A white dove rises from a dirty sill
and perches on a gargoyle's broken nose.

Trees, Walking

In deep, deep autumn when the last leaves lie
beneath the barren limbs of skeletons,
leaning westward in the blast and eye
of a storm, as if walking where the sun's

rays blaze on, in the gospels of the mind,
amid the tattered pages of Saint Mark,
you find yourself no longer fully blind,
following the evangelists, the bark

of their robes still touched by the holy word,
their mortal Teacher not too far ahead,
where winter's followed by a singing bird,
and leaves are resurrected from the dead.

To Love This Flesh

To love this flesh,
its rivers and valleys,
its fruits,
ripe or rotting.

To be conscious,
to understand a toad's agony
or delight.

To finger the pricks of a bush,
lick the blood of the world
with a warm tongue,
and comprehend a crow's hunger.

To breathe the spring air
full of laughing and weeping,
like a sow thistle
or lazy lizard.

To endure
without any sense of time—
to wake, sleep, live and die
under the same sun, moon and stars,
eternal as a weed.

To love the rhythm of this being,
like sperm swimming upstream
in one you love,

never questioning
or doubting the gods.

Tobias to His Angel

"All was taken away from you: white dresses,
wings, even existence.
Yet I believe in you,
messengers."
—Czesław Miłosz

They say you don't exist,
that when you come at night,
it is the curtain, light

upon my trembling wrist,
that saves me from despair,
that it is I who bear

the burden; I who pull
the trigger; I who wrest
the pistol from my chest.

They say you can't console
and that in truth I stride
alone without a guide.

I don't know even now
as wind blows through the curtain
and hope begins to burgeon,
who touched my lowered brow.

Tombstone

In memory of Maryann Mercurio

I do not think I have to tell you, Joey,
how the seasons multiplied, and smothered
your family's final holdouts, hilltops snowy
in the blue-lit backdrop behind your mother's
blazing hair, her slouched and aching shoulders
at rest now at the ending of her story,
how the sunshine trickled down, the boulder
moved away, the flowers whispered "glory."

Ultima Thule

for Cornel Adam Lengyel (1915–2003)

It is a day like any other day.
Bullfinches bathe in dust along the path.
Two hedgehogs mate. A crow attempts to sing.
The cherries bloom until you see an orchard
and in a puddle snowdrops touch the sky.
Then, when you least expect, you reach your goal.
Your heart stops, and you fall towards your shadow.

Ulysses

His head reels—gulls beneath the mackerel sky
prey on schools of pilchards, sprats, and herrings.
He holds the helm fast, tries to catch his bearings
in the mirror of a bloodshot eye.

A tempest bellows, "All clouds lead to Rome.
Light pours down on both the preyed and preying."
Grateful for the dark, the light and greying,
he spurns his ache and calls the moment home.

Unity Mitford

*"She learned to walk again, but never fully recovered.
She was incontinent and childish."*

She had sat at the Chancellor's feet, a rival
to Eva Braun, highborn, blue-eyed, contrary
to the reds, dykes and faggots of Bloomsbury,
armed with only Campbell's *Flowering Rifle*.
Surely she'd been guilty of high treason?
(Albion is a better place today,
a heaven for the black man and the gay!)
Nevertheless, this was not the reason
she chose not to renew her yearly lease,
weeping at the news of London's choice.
(There would be a pearl-handled pistol's noise
days after the end of unhardy peace.)
No, not the reason few recall her name,
or, afterwards, why she was not the same.

Visiting My Dead Grandmother's Cottage with My Father in the Forests of Lithuania: 1966

Visiting her cottage I remember ripe ears of corn,
drawers full of bent knives, mouldy crusts of pumper-
nickel bread,
high shelves of hoary berry jams, curtains threadbare and
torn,
and an axe brighter than the cracks in the wall near a
bed
bereft of her broken body for three months and one
week.
Through a veranda window I recall a thistled yard,
and still hear portents issuing from a fat raven's beak.
A bucket of stagnant water mirrors the cloudy lard
she must have fried eggs and coffee grinds in every
morning.
And by a potato patch I see a wild war-like pig,
with its head full of demons, palavering and snorting.
And I shout something and ineptly cast a birch's twig
while my father speaks to an old peasant in a strange
tongue
about pagan deities carved on trees when he was young.

Wake

The cactus pricks the window pane,
the withered rose begs for a drink.
You look down at the red borscht stain
upon her apron, and you think:

never again will she light stoves
with a wood match, or kindle coal,
never again will she hoard loaves,
or spread *pâté* on a stale roll.

Seven weeks after Easter, face
now waxed and powdered for the worms,
she waits for God at her own pace
as you attempt to come to terms.

All here defies the resurrection:
the borscht-stained apron, the withered rose,
the cactus leaning with affection
towards the only light it knows.

Wake Cake

You fly back home, sit at the kitchen table
with the wake cake. The crumbs inside the foil.
Thirty years have passed and you are able
only to stare outside. You watch him toil
in the garden, turn the frozen soil.
You open up his lager, pick the label,
look at the food that in three days will spoil,
wonder if there is meaning to the fable.
He rests the rusty shovel by the window.
His heavy breath is warm and live and rising.
He smiles to you. You feel the winter wind blow
through the panes. You look down at the icing.
He's speaking now beyond the stars. You listen.
You are ten years old and forever his son.

Water

Burnt Sudanese earth under claw,
a vulture waits three steps behind
a girl who crouches, strands of straw
beneath her lowered head, her mind

in refuge on the dream-kissed shores
of an oasis, where green palm
leaves shade black brows, and water pours
into a pool that's bright but calm

A flame-tree sheds no grief, instead
droops in the backdrop. A stump lies
resembling a lion's head
still warding off the thirst of flies.

When Nothing Remains

For Kasia

Today, I think, I'd like to have you pose
surrounded by abundant store and riches,
surrounded by elaborate head-dresses,
water-heavy pearls and silken hose.

I want you in the dark, holding a rose,
among bronzes, candlesticks and vases,
vases from which a balmy steam arises
into a Great Dane's dilating nose.

Rembrandt, doubtless, must have felt this way
when painting Saskia in a velvet gown
as she approached her death before his sight—

as if with grapes he could prolong her stay,
as if he wished to weigh her beauty down
with the luminescent heft of candlelight.

TRANSLATIONS

Asters

Asters—sweltering days,
old entreaty, spell,
the gods shed timid rays,
an hour upon the scale.

Once more the golden flocks,
the sky, the light, the veil.
What breeds the familiar flux
of wings before they fail?

Once more now the lust,
the rush of roses, and you—
the summer's leaned to watch
the swallows skirt the dew,

and once more does not falter,
sure dark precedes new light:
the swallows drink the water
and fade into the night.

—after the German of Gottfried Benn
(1886–1956)

An Autumn Evening

The brown village. A darkness often treads
Along the walls that stand in autumn. Mock-
Shapes: man as well as woman, dead now, walk
In the cold parlours to prepare their beds.

Here young boys play. A heavy shadow spreads
Over brown dung. Servant women walk
Through the moist blue, and sometimes their eyes mock
It, longing, as bells toll above their heads.

An inn leans for the down and lonely there.
Patiently it waits beneath dark arches,
Moved by clouds of gold tobacco smoke,

Yet always black and near. A stranger soaked
In booze stands in the shade of older arches
After the wild birds take to the air.

—after the German of Georg Trakl (1887–1914)

Apollo's Archaic Torso

We have no knowledge of his ancient brow
where pippins ripen. Yet his torso gleams,
reflecting the candela, luminous streams
that yet pour from his gaze, his glance's glow

still radiant, though dimmed. If not, his bare
breast would not blind you in the silent turn
of hip and thighs, a smile not flash and burn
through groins, his genitals not ever glare.

If not, this stone would seem deformed and small,
the light beneath his shoulder's sudden fall
not seem a preying panther's shimmering mane,

not burst beyond the limits of the skies,
starlike, until there is no point or plane
blind to your ways. You must change your life.

—*after the German of Rainer Maria Rilke (1875–1926)*

149

Black, Black Rooks

Black, black rooks, where, whence do you fly
Here in my garden how fast you die

Here near my feeder by my jays
O rooks! How being's blackness stays

And what dark claws and what great bill
Here in my garden the depths are real

For warblers and doves I am a riddle
What was I thinking when I was little

I thought being a toy amid hedgerows
Here by my sparrows, doves and crows

—*after the Polish of Jarosław Marek Rymkiewicz (1935–)*

Carol

They come slowly—loiter, you might say,
Some with olive oil splashed on their bums,
Others with enormous crooked thumbs,
All full of holes like sculptures on display.

Broads . . . up to their elbows in sweet cake;
Widows . . . clad in blizzards of mock snow;
Ladies . . . so thin that their skeletons glow;
Tarts . . . with three nights of fasting in their wake.

Animals: a goat, two rooks, a camel,
(A camel from the ZOO with a pierced lip),
A spitz that wears a ribbon and a slip,
A raven perched on some strange nameless mammal.

The three kings last: one with a face of gauze,
The second with a jaw made out of plaster,
The third as beautiful as alabaster,
Though his crown's sharper than the teeth of saws.

They stand and watch. The mother, mid trees, swings,
Sprawled out, her feet rocking back and forth.
Sometimes a drop of silence hits the floor,
Sometimes a mouse squeaks, or a stone sings.

How long can the foetus keep flesh mired? How
long can the star fall in our marrows?
Sometimes a mouse squeaks, or boulder carols,
And this is all, so far, that has transpired . . .

—*after the Polish of Stanisław Grochowiak (1934–1976)*

151

December 1942

How resounding is the winter squall.
Hole-riddled the loam walls of Bethlehem's stall.

That's Mary murdered at the entrance gate,
Hair frozen to the bloody stones and grate.

Masked in rags, three soldiers limping by
Cannot burn from her ear the infant's cry.

The last canteen sunflower won't get them far.
They seek the way and cannot see the star.

Aurum, thus, myrrham offerunt . . .
Crow and cur come to a manger ruined.

. . . quia natus est nobis Dominus.
On a bleached skeleton gleam soot and ooze.

The way to Stalingrad's a smouldering glow.
And it leads to a charnel house of snow.

—after the German of Peter Huchel (1903–1981)

Killing Fish

What's she crying about—this old crone eaten away by salt,
This poor sick woman with a petunia in her at two?
And why's this fish doing somersaults
Amid fragile lipsticks and scattered rouge?

And why does she keep staring at the fish like that,
What's its sickly mouth trying to tell her?
Why are old lipsticks fragile and cracked,
And powdered rouge paler and paler?

—*after the Polish of Stanisław Grochowiak (1934–1976)*

Last Spring

Take the forsythias deep within, each leaf,
and when the lilac blossoms on the lawn,
mix it, too, with your blood and joy and grief,
the dark soil that you depend upon.

Sluggish days. All have been gotten through.
And if you do not ask: the start or close,
then perhaps the hours will carry you
as distantly as June's unfolding rose.

—after the German of Gottfried Benn (1886–1956)

Night

Night, street, lamp, and pharmacy,
A meaningless and misty light.
Live on a quarter century—
The same. There is no hope of flight.

You will die, rise from where you fell,
All be repeated, cold and damp:
The night, the wavering canal,
The pharmacy, the street, the lamp.

*—after the Russian of Alexander Blok (1888–
1921)*

The Akkerman Steppe

I launch myself across the dry and open narrows,
My carriage plunging into green as if a ketch,
Floundering through the meadow flowers in the stretch.
I pass an archipelago of coral yarrows.

It's dusk now, not a road in sight, nor ancient barrows.
I look up at the sky and look for stars to catch.
There distant clouds glint—there tomorrow starts to etch;
The Dnieper glimmers; Akkerman's lamp shines and harrows.

I stand in stillness, hear the migratory cranes,
Their necks and wings beyond the reach of preying hawks;
Hear where the sooty copper glides across the plains,

Where on its underside a viper writhes through stalks.
Amid the hush I lean my ears down grassy lanes
And listen for a voice from home. Nobody talks.

—after the Polish of Adam Mickiewicz (1798–1855)

The Birch

The birch beneath
My windowsill
Stands like a wreath
In the silver chill

Of winter, white
In the faint glow
Of early light
And softest snow.

The birch still yields
Stars at this time,
Though over fields
Sun breaks through rime.

Dawn wakes the grounds
And sleeping ploughs,
But makes its rounds
Through silver boughs.

—after the Russian of Sergei Yesenin (1895–1925)

The Calm of the Sea
Upon the height of Tarkankut

The pennant at the crow's nest rises with the breeze,
Shafts of sunlight play upon the water's breast
As on a bride-to-be who wakes to sigh and rest,
And wakes again and sighs for dreams that better please.

On naked spars the banner-shaped sails hang at ease.
The vessel is in chains now, leeside facing west,
Lulled by slow rocking. Passengers lampoon in jest,
Swabbies sigh to one another, slapping knees.

Blithe Sea! Among your jolly living creatures is
The polyp, sleeping in your depths when dark clouds swarm,
Wielding longish arms amid each starfish grave.

Sweet dreams! Below a hydra of remembrances
Sleeps in the middle of mishaps and raging storm,
And when the heart is calm, its pincers flash and wave.

—*after the Polish of Adam Mickiewicz (1798–1855)*

The Castle Ruins at Balaklava

These castles, whose remains are strewn in heaps for miles,
Once graced and guarded you, Crimea the ungrateful!
Today they sit upon the hills, each like a great skull
In which reptiles reside or men worse than reptiles.

Let's climb a tower, search for crests upon worn tiles,
For an inscription or a hero's name, the fateful
Bane of armies now forgotten by the faithful,
A wizened beetle wrapped in vines below the aisles.

Here Greeks wrought Attic ornaments upon the walls,
From which Italians would cast Mongols into chains,
And where the Mecca-bound once stopped to pray and beg.

Today above the tombs the shadow of night falls,
The black-winged buzzards fly like pennants over plains,
As if towards a city ever touched by plague.

—*after the Polish of Adam Mickiewicz (1798–1855)*

Chatyr Dah

The trembling Muslims kiss your foot and pray out loud,
O mast of the Crimean tall ship Chatyr Dah,
Minaret amid the hills and Padishah!
You, having fled above the cliffs into a cloud,

Stand at the gates of heaven, humbling the crowd,
And, like great Gabriel, guard lost Eden's house, your shaw
Of trees a cloak where janissaries keep the law,
Your turban thunderbolts and lightning for the proud.

And yet sun scolds our brows and fog obscures our ways,
Locusts poach our crops and Gavur burn our homes,
Always, Chatyr Dah, as motionless as domes

In Mecca, you remain indifferent to our days,
Creation's dragoman to what below you roams
Who only hears whatever God to nature says.

—*after the Polish of Adam Mickiewicz (1798–1855)*

The Dream

High noon in Dagestan, I lay marooned
In blistering heat, a bullet in my breast.
Smoke still rose in the valley from my wound
As drop-by-drop I watched blood flowing west.

I lay upon the loam of that strange land,
Cliffs closing in, the sun soon touching peaks,
Reaching past the mountain with its hand
To burn my dreaming brow and death-pale cheeks.

I dreamt I saw the flaming orb's bright glare
Feasting on poppies in my native parts,
And braided girls with flowers in their hair,
Recalling me with soft hands on their hearts.

But in the oaken table's hazy gleam
I saw another girl with half-crazed eyes.
She sat as if a captive in a dream,
Her stare the shade or shroud of starless skies.

She dreamt of that strange place in Dagestan,
Of smoke ascending over the black breast
Of a strange but somehow familiar man
As drop-by-drop he watched blood flowing west.

—after the Russian of Mikhail Lermontov (1814–1841)

The Moment

What matter that it's passing? That it passes?
Moments exist if only to pass by,
Hardly mine, no longer anyone else's,
Like cloudy masterpieces in the sky.

Though everything perpetually changes,
And moments are replaced by moments waiting,
Always in lakes among the masterpieces
Either stars or pretty girls are bathing.

—after the Polish of Leopold Staff (1878–1957)

The Past

1.

God does not make the p a s t, nor death, nor grief,
But he who breaks the law,
Whose depths are so raw,
He, knowing evil, seeks a m n e s i a for relief.

2.

However, he's not like a child inside a stroller,
Crying: "Look, there's a tree,
Only to see it flee . . .
Into the woods!"; the tree remains; the child grows older.

3.

The past exists today as well as beyond the green:
A simple hamlet waits
Not this or that odd place . . .
Whose fields no living man has ever walked or seen.

—*after the Polish of Cyprian Kamil Norwid (1821–1883)*

The Sail

A lonely sail moves, white on white,
Amid the ocean's mist and foam.
Caught now in a distant light,
What does it seek so far from home?

The halyards groan, the mast-beam creaks;
The sail now billows in the breeze.
It is not happiness it seeks,
Nor happiness from which it flees.

Above, the sun is blithe and warm;
Below, the blue waves rise and crest.
The rebel searches for a storm
As if in storms it could find rest.

—after the Russian of Mikhail Lermontov (1814–1841)

ABOUT THE AUTHOR

Leo Yankevich was born into a family of Roman Catholic Irish-Polish immigrants on October 30, 1961. He grew up and attended high school in Farrell, Pennsylvania, a small steel town in the Rust Belt of Middle America. He then studied History and Polish at Alliance College, Cambridge Springs, Penn., receiving a BA in 1984. Later that year he travelled to Poland on a fellowship to study at the centuries-old Jagiellonian University in Krakow. A staunch anti-communist, he played an active role in the dissident movement in that country. He was arrested and beaten badly on a few occasions by the communist security forces. After the fall of the Iron Curtain in 1989, he decided to settle permanently in Poland. Since that time he has lived in Gliwice (Gleiwitz), an industrial city in Upper Silesia.